Dr. LaDonna C. Osborn

Jesus
&WOMEN

Answers to Three Big Questions

Bible quotations in this book are from the New King James Version unless otherwise noted. Other languages and versions have been considered. Scriptures may be personalized, paraphrased, abridged or conformed to the person and tense of their contextual application, to foster clarity and individual acceptance. Chapter and verse references enable the reader to verify accuracy.

All Scripture is from the *New King James Version*, Copyright © 1982 by Thomas Nelson, Inc.

Jesus & Women: Answers to Three Big Questions
ISBN 0-87943-109-1
Copyright © 2000 by LaDonna C. Osborn
Printed in the United States of America.
All rights reserved.

Published by OSFO Publishers
P.O. Box 10, Tulsa, OK 74102 USA

OSFO International
P.O. Box 10, Tulsa, OK 74102 USA
918-743-6231 • FAX 918-749-0339
Email: OSFO@aol.com • www.osborn.org

Canada: Box 281, Adelaide St. Post Sta., Toronto M5C 2J4
England: Box 148, Birmingham B3 2LG
(a registered charity)

Contents

Introduction

My purpose in publishing this
sermon is simple:

> *I want you to have
> an encounter with Jesus.*

We are living in a time that is experi-
encing dramatic changes. One change
concerns the value and the roles of
women. Both the church and society
are struggling to determine the proper
place for women. Questions are being
asked that must be answered. It is my
belief that the only source for valid
answers to such questions is the
Person of Jesus Christ. How did He
view women? What did He expect
of them? How did He answer the

questions about women while He was here
on earth?

As you read this booklet, you may have an
encounter with Jesus that answers some of the
questions you, too, have been asking. His answers
to questions always offer hope, dignity, and purpose
to the individual lives of women and men.

On the pages that follow, we will look at three
different encounters that Jesus had with women.
Each woman represents a unique category of
women who live today. Each of these dramatic
encounters between Jesus and a woman suggests
a question that is being asked today. In each
example we will discover Jesus' answer to a big
question that will reshape our present attitudes
about ourselves as women and about others who
are yearning to discover their own dignity
through identity with Jesus Christ.

1

JESUS &
The Sinful Woman

John 8:1-12

But Jesus went to the Mount of Olives. Now early in the morning He came again into the temple, and all the people came to Him; and He sat down and taught them. Then the scribes and Pharisees brought to Him a woman caught in adultery. And when they had set her in the midst, they said to Him, "Teacher, this woman was caught in adultery, in the very act. Now Moses, in the law, commanded us that such should be stoned. But what do

You say?" This they said, testing Him, that they might have something of which to accuse Him.

But Jesus stooped down and wrote on the ground with His finger, as though He did not hear. So when they continued asking Him, He raised Himself up and said to them, "He who is without sin among you, let him throw a stone at her first." And again He stooped down and wrote on the ground.

Then those who heard it, being convicted by their conscience, went out one by one, beginning with the oldest even to the last. And Jesus was left alone, and the woman standing in the midst. When Jesus had raised Himself up and saw no one but the woman, He said to her, "Woman, where are those accusers of yours? Has no one condemned you?"

She said, "No one, Lord."

> *And Jesus said to her, "Neither do I condemn you; go and sin no more." Then Jesus spoke to them again, saying, "I am the light of the world. He who follows Me shall not walk in darkness, but have the light of life."*

This story records an encounter that Jesus had with a woman who was obviously guilty of sexual promiscuity. She was dragged by the religious leaders, the scribes and Pharisees, into the presence of Jesus while He was teaching in the synagogue. They announced that this woman had been caught in the act of adultery. Notice that they did not bring her to Jesus because they were concerned about her life as a person. They were only using her circumstance as an opportunity to accuse Jesus of breaking a Mosaic law. The sinful woman was rather a means to an end.

The religious leaders said, "This woman was caught in the very act of adultery. Moses and the law say such should be stoned. But what do *you* say?"

Their question gets my attention. Although their question is rooted in a wrong motive, they did ask a good question. They asked Jesus, "What do you say?" Jesus did not answer them in words. The scripture says that He stooped down and began to write on the ground. We do not know what He wrote, but apparently every eye was captivated by Christ's actions. Gradually every man – from the oldest to the youngest – who had gathered to accuse the woman, began to leave. After every accuser had left, the scripture says that Jesus was left there with the woman.

Then Jesus, who had stooped down to write, raised Himself up to address the woman. I love the verbal imagery that is drawn as Jesus stoops down, where the woman had probably been thrown. This reminds me that Jesus, as God in the flesh, comes to where we are and identifies with our condition. He is not ashamed to identify with sinful people. He comes to us at the very point of our crisis and our despair.

The scripture says that when He stood up

again, all of the woman's accusers were gone.
He was alone with the sinful woman. Jesus looked
at the woman and He said, "Where are those
accusers of yours? Isn't there anyone?" She must
have looked around in amazement to see that
Jesus had already begun to deal with her problem.
She answered Him, "No one, Lord." Then He
said to her, "Woman, neither do I condemn you.
Go and sin no more." Then Jesus added, "I am
the light of the world. The one who follows me
will not walk in darkness, but will have the
light of life."

THE | QUESTION
What are we going to do with the women?

Because of my broad international ministry
involvement, I am exposed to various cultures
and traditions, both secular and religious.

Because of the current emphasis on issues that concern women, there seems to be an underlying question wherever I go that reminds me of the encounter between Jesus and the sinful woman. The question is, *What are we going to do with the women?* We cannot ignore them. We cannot excommunicate them. We cannot suppress them. We cannot control them. We cannot do without them. We definitely need them. *But what are we going to do with the women?*

What is the church going to do with women (and men) who make mistakes, who sin?

Everyone makes mistakes. You do. I do. We, as the Church, must reconsider our attitudes and actions toward people who do things that are not right. Too often, when a person violates one of God's commands we are quick to condemn. However, our response should be the same as Christ's response. Jesus' example always puts issues into the right perspective.

We must remember that we are not to condemn those who have made mistakes. The scripture says that Jesus was not sent into the world to condemn the world, but that the world, through Him, might be saved. (John 3:17) We who represent Jesus Christ in the earth today are to be among the company of non-condemners.

I want you to know that Jesus has an answer for everyone who has ever made a mistake or sinned. As you read this, you may be living with the weight of guilt as the result of a mistake that you made. You may have secrets that haunt you. You may not know who to talk to, in your church or among your friends, fearing that you may be rejected, excommunicated, or disallowed from serving in some capacity. You may think you have a mark against you that can never be removed.

I tell you today that Jesus' answer to you is not one of condemnation, rather it is one of invitation.

THE | ANSWER
*Give them
a new beginning.*

To those who make mistakes, Jesus gives
a new beginning. We should always be ready to
give *a new beginning* to anyone who has made
a mistake. Of course, when we do that we may be
accused of compromising, of being naive, of being
used, or of letting people take advantage of us. We
are to live by Christ's example and value system,
rather than by the standards of society. The Lord
Jesus Christ has established our standard. He
came to seek and save the lost. (Luke 19:10) That
is our mission, also.

Remember, rather than condemning the
sinful woman, Jesus offered her *a new beginning.*
He said, "I am the light of the world. Whoever
follows me will never walk in darkness but will
have the light of life." (John 8:12 NRSV) His
answer to people with a sinful past is to give

a new beginning and to invite them to follow Him. Where light is, darkness cannot stay. Remaining close to Jesus deals with the darkness which tries to engulf and enslave people.

Jesus offers the same *new beginning* to you, to me, and to every other woman (or man) who has made a mistake. The closer we are to Jesus, the brighter His light shines in and through our lives as we give personal witness of His grace and His power to redeem.

2

JESUS &

The Imperfect Woman

Luke 13:10-17

Now He was teaching in one of the synagogues on the Sabbath. And behold, there was a woman who had a spirit of infirmity eighteen years, and was bent over and could in no way raise herself up. But when Jesus saw her, He called her to Him and said to her, "Woman, you are loosed from your infirmity." And He laid His hands on her, and immediately she was made straight, and glorified God.

But the ruler of the synagogue

answered with indignation, because
Jesus had healed on the Sabbath; and he
said to the crowd, "There are six days on
which men ought to work; therefore come
and be healed on them, and not on the
Sabbath day."

The Lord then answered him and
said, "Hypocrite! Does not each one of
you on the Sabbath loose his ox or donkey
from the stall, and lead it away to water
it? So ought not this woman, being a
daughter of Abraham, whom Satan has
bound; think of it; for eighteen years, be
loosed from this bond on the Sabbath?"
And when He said these things, all His
adversaries were put to shame; and all the
multitude rejoiced for all the glorious
things that were done by Him.

The second question is based on an encounter that a crippled woman had with Jesus. We see that Jesus is again teaching in the synagogue. It is interesting to me that these questions seem to arise in the very places where the answers should be the most obvious. The words and attitudes of Christ should be expressed through every Christian believer, each biblical sermon, and each encounter by the Church with hurting people.

By this time in the development of Judaism, the synagogue had taken on characteristics not found in the tabernacle pattern given by God during the Israelites' journey in the wilderness. The temple constructed by Herod included segregated areas for certain types of people. For example, in the synagogue where Jesus was teaching, there was a Women's Court where the women gathered to hear the teachings.

This type of division, or segregation, was not God's plan in the beginning. We see in the first chapter of Genesis that God created both male and female in His own image and gave both male and

female blessing and instruction. (Genesis 1:26-30)
God's beautiful plan of inclusiveness, of community,
of family, is so often marred and divided by the
sinful hands of men and women. In many parts
of the world today, women are still not allowed to
fully participate in the plan of God, as He intended
in the beginning.

Why were the women kept at a distance?
Why do we restrict some people today? Is God's
Word so fragile that those who are viewed as
different cannot get close because they may do
certain damage to it? Of course not. It is the very
Word of God that brings healing to every human
condition. God sends His Word and causes what-
ever was broken to be made whole again.

So here we see Jesus teaching, and the scripture
says that He saw a woman. Now we have no
record that anything happened to draw His attention to this woman, other than by the very Spirit
of God that was in Him. We know she was not
near Him because she, as female, would have
been in the distant Women's Court. Also, those

who had any type of deformity or imperfection were segregated.

The scripture says that the woman was bent over, and had been in that condition for 18 years. In this woman, we can see a picture of humanity with all of its imperfections. When Jesus saw her, He called to her and said, "Woman, be loosed from your infirmity." (Luke 13:12) The religious leaders who were clinging to the Law, and who were more interested in the rules on paper than in the purpose of God in flesh, reacted with the attitude, "Oh, no. He can't do that today. That is not on the program."

Jesus' response was swift and searing: "You hypocrites! ...ought not this woman, being a daughter of Abraham, whom Satan has bound... be loosed from this bond on the Sabbath?" (Luke 13:15-16)

THE | QUESTION
Why bother with the women?

During my travels, I have seen women like this all over the world. They carry heavy loads that eventually destroy their bodies, often bending their backs double. I have seen them strap cloths around their foreheads and fill them with wood or heavy objects until the load seems unbearable. These dear women carry their loads, stooped low, trying to use their backs as leverage to support the weight. Their labors are vital in supplying their families and communities with the necessities of life. These women do this so long that when they become old they remain stooped, even when they are not carrying a load.

I have such compassion for these women because once they are broken down, they are of no further use in their communities. They were broken by the weight of circumstance, by the demands of their societies, and by the inferiority of their roles in life. Yet, I see them the way I believe God sees them: they are His human creation, in bondage, and He wants them to be loosed. Although they are imperfect in the eyes of their societies, they are beautiful in His eyes.

Like these women, you may be weighted down by your own circumstances. You may feel that, because you are a woman, you have an inferior role in life. You may feel that your life is worthless and others are asking the question: *Why bother with the women?*

THE | ANSWER
Give them
a new identity.

Jesus' answer is not one of rejection, but one of affirmation. He called her *daughter.* Every woman, regardless of her appearance or what she may have to offer, is a daughter of God, created in His image, with a predestined and divine purpose. Women are valuable to God because they are part of His image in the earth. Their value is not based on what they can do or how many babies they can have. It is not in their monetary affluence, their status in society, or in the strength of their backs. Their value is in their innate humanity as God's expression in physical form.

Why bother with the women? Because humanity belongs to God. The Kingdom of God is made of things that are not always valued by temporal society. The purposes of the Kingdom of God begin with understanding the value of people. You may be feeling unimportant and useless today. Be encouraged! Because you are a human person, you have an identity that elevates you above all the rest of creation and sets you high in a position of great worth and dignity. God came in Christ to restore you to this place of purpose. His message to you, through the Gospel, is that your value is not based on your *imperfections,* but on Christ's *perfection*.

You are valuable. It does not matter what you can give, but rather who you are. And because of who you are, the Great One desires to come into you and take up His abode. The scripture says "...to all who receive Him, who believe in His name, He gives power to become children of God..." (John 1:12)

Jesus is not only saying to this woman in the Bible, "Daughter, be loosed," He is also saying it to you right now. You are His daughter, so be loosed today from everything that binds you, from everything that holds you back, and from everything that puts you down. See Jesus as the one who lifts you up, and hold on to that vision.

3

JESUS &
The Rejected Woman

John 4:4-35

But He needed to go through Samaria. So He came to a city of Samaria which is called Sychar, near the plot of ground that Jacob gave to his son Joseph. Now Jacob's well was there. Jesus therefore, being wearied from His journey, sat thus by the well. It was about the sixth hour.

A woman of Samaria came to draw water. Jesus said to her, "Give Me a drink." For His disciples had gone away into the city to buy food.

Then the woman of Samaria said to Him, "How is it that You, being a Jew, ask a drink from me, a Samaritan woman?" For Jews have no dealings with Samaritans.

Jesus answered and said to her, "If you knew the gift of God, and who it is who says to you, 'Give Me a drink,' you would have asked Him, and He would have given you living water."

The woman said to Him, "Sir, You have nothing to draw with, and the well is deep. Where then do You get that living water? Are You greater than our father Jacob, who gave us the well, and drank from it himself, as well as his sons and his livestock?"

Jesus answered and said to her, "Whoever drinks of this water will thirst again, but whoever drinks of the water that I shall give him will never thirst. But the water that I shall give him will become in him a fountain of water springing up into everlasting life."

The woman said to Him, "Sir, give me this water, that I may not thirst, nor come here to draw." Jesus said to her, "Go, call your husband, and come here."

The woman answered and said, "I have no husband."

Jesus said to her, "You have well said, 'I have no husband,' for you have had five husbands, and the one whom you now have is not your husband; in that you spoke truly."

The woman said to Him, "Sir, I perceive that You are a prophet. Our fathers worshipped on this mountain, and you Jews say that in Jerusalem is the place where one ought to worship."

Jesus said to her, "Woman, believe Me, the hour is coming when you will neither on this mountain, nor in Jerusalem, worship the Father. You worship what you do not know; we know what we worship, for salvation is of the Jews. But the hour is coming, and now is, when the true worshipers will worship the Father in spirit and truth; for the Father is seeking such to worship Him. God is Spirit, and those who worship Him must worship in spirit and truth."

The woman said to Him, "I know that Messiah is coming" (who is called Christ). "When He comes, He will tell us all things."

Jesus said to her, "I who speak to you am He."

And at this point His disciples came, and they marveled that He talked with a woman; yet no one said, "What do You seek?" or, "Why are You talking with her?"

The woman then left her waterpot, went her way into the city, and said to the men, "Come, see a Man who told me all things that I ever did. Could this be the Christ?" Then they went out of the city and came to Him.

In the meantime His disciples urged Him, saying, "Rabbi, eat."

> But He said to them, "I have food
> to eat of which you do not know."
>
> Therefore the disciples said to one
> another, "Has anyone brought Him any-
> thing to eat?"
>
> Jesus said to them, "My food is to
> do the will of Him who sent Me, and to
> finish His work. Do you not say, 'There
> are still four months and then comes the
> harvest'? Behold, I say to you, lift up
> your eyes and look at the fields, for they
> are already white for harvest!"

Our third account of a woman's encounter
with Jesus is a familiar story. The scripture says
that Jesus *needed* to go through Samaria. I like this
story because we see Jesus outside the synagogue,
relating to people in everyday life. The woman
was a Samaritan, not a Jew. Her status as a woman,
her race as a Samaritan, and her circumstance as a
woman without a valid family all compounded
against her. She was a rejected woman. In this

encounter between Jesus and the rejected woman, we see that Jesus took the initiative, went to her and spoke to her. She asked for nothing, but Jesus cared about her.

As we consider John's record of Jesus' encounter with this woman, we must think beyond the negative picture that has often been painted in sermons about this dear woman. Let's assume that she was getting water at a time of day when the well was not busy. Perhaps she did not feel good about herself, and was tired of the glances, the innuendoes, and possibly the accusations and remarks that may have followed her. She probably just wanted to be left alone by the well on that day.

As the woman approached the well and saw the Jewish man sitting there, she had no reason to expect Him to say anything to her. Now why would a Jewish Rabbi talk to a woman in the first place? Why would He talk to a Samaritan? Why would He talk about the holy things of faith and worship with her? And why would He ask her such a personal question? When He delved into the most personal and bruised areas of her heart it must have seemed to her that He was peeling away everything that had served as a defense against the rejections of people.

Jesus said, "Go, call your husband, and come here." She answered "I don't have a husband." Jesus' candid answer was, "You've told the truth." As preachers, I think we should present this text more often in a way that affirms the character of this woman. If His question was a test, she passed. Then He began to "tell her all that she ever did." (John 4:29)

He said, "You have told the truth. You have had five husbands and the one that you are with now is not your husband." (John 4:17-18). Something in her heart must have begun to churn, but not because of guilt or the fear of exposure (as has been taught). She must have looked into His eyes and thought to herself, "This man is different. He knows about me. He knows my pain and he knows my shame. He knows it all, and yet he is talking to me."

Then something remarkable happened. The woman recognized that Jesus was someone special, possibly a prophet. They had a discussion about whether God should be worshipped on the mountain in Samaria or in Jerusalem. She expressed her conclusion by saying, "I know that Messiah is coming...When He comes, He will tell us all things." Then Jesus declared, "I who speak to you am He." (John 4:25-26)

THE | QUESTION
Why talk to the women?

This same question has come down through the ages, and there are people today, both in and out of the church, asking, "*Why talk to the women?* They do not have anything to say. They can not be trusted. They should stay in their place. They will cause problems."

Jesus came to the woman when no one else wanted to talk to her. The scripture says that when the disciples arrived, they marveled at the fact that He was talking with a woman. I can just see their faces, with their eyes getting bigger as they talked among themselves, wondering what He was doing, asking "Why is He talking to the woman?"

The woman left her water pot and ran to town where she began to announce, "Come, see a Man who told me all things that I ever did. Could this be the Christ?" (John 4:29) Notice that she ran from the disciples, but she ran to the world that needed Jesus.

The scripture says that because of this woman, the town came out to see Jesus. But notice at that moment, the disciples were more interested in having lunch than in observing the miracle of Jesus' encounter with the rejected woman. Jesus said to them, "My food is to do the will of Him who sent me...lift up your eyes and look at the fields, for they are already white for harvest!" (John 4:34-35) At that moment, we see Jesus' heart yearning toward those who are the rejected of this world.

I tell women all over the world that if the men will not accept them or their ministry, they can go to the world of hurting people that is ready to receive their message of hope, healing, and life in Christ. You may have been rejected by society or by religious tradition. Because of your past, you may feel disqualified to do anything important for God. You may believe that there are those who would look at you and say *Why talk to this woman?* But Jesus' ways are not the world's ways, and He has the answer for you today.

THE | ANSWER
Give them a new purpose.

Purpose is what Christianity is all about. It is not about rules, status, or position. Christianity is about the eternal purpose for which all people were created. It is a purpose for which we are reborn and into which we are baptized. Christianity is the person and the mission of Christ, personified in people today.

Each woman (or man) who believes in Christ becomes His ambassador of Good News to her world of influence. Regardless of our rejected status in the world, when we accept Jesus Christ, He trusts us as carriers of His life. The woman of Samaria became a voice of hope in her community as her unimportant life became one of great purpose. When we understand that Christ's own life is at work through us, we will become bold reapers of the people-harvest that belongs to God.

I can think of no greater statement to make to you than this: whether you are a young woman or a great-grandmother, accept today the new beginning that God is offering to you. Accept His identity upon you so you might take hold of His purpose for your life. You can make a difference in your world.

When we talk about Jesus and women today, we see that neither His attitude nor His answers to our questions have changed. Those who have made mistakes are to be offered a new beginning. Those who seem to have nothing to contribute are to be offered a new identity. And those who are seen as rejects from society or from our hallowed halls are to be given a new purpose.

4

JESUS &
The Redeemed Woman

A Story From Today:
The Woman in Kenya

In 1996, I was preaching in a crusade in Kisumu, Kenya, East Africa. I will never forget the face of a woman who had walked 48 hours with her little girl to come to that crusade in order to be healed. The woman was dying of AIDS.

She would walk for a while, and then have to lay by the side of the road to rest. I do not have to tell you that the very condition that she carried in her body caused her to be segregated from her family and from the community. She was viewed as unclean and she was labeled as immoral. Her entire life was devastated.

However, in that hopeless condition, the woman believed that if she could get to Kisumu, to a place where Jesus was being preached, a place where there was prayer and faith, there could be hope for her. She heard the gospel, believed on Christ, and was marvelously healed by Christ's power.

Now, the question could easily be, *"How do you know?* You have to get a blood test. Did you administer a blood test on the platform? You mean you just let her testify and you assumed she was healed?" Yes, I believed that she was healed. She had strength and vitality and faith in Christ.

She testified publicly that she had been healed. Although I could see that she was skin and bones, there was a beautiful twinkle in her eyes that was not her own. It was the life of Christ in her, and His resurrection was very evident in her mortal flesh.

It has now been several years since that crusade, and I recently returned to Kenya where I saw the most precious thing. This same little woman came, but she was not skinny. At first I did not recognize her. When she was introduced to me, they said, "Do you remember the woman who came in 1996 and was healed of AIDS?" When I saw this precious woman she was all plumped up, but she had the same vitality of Christ's life that I had seen years earlier.

The woman had already planted three churches in Kenya and she continues to be a living witness that Jesus Christ has not changed. (Hebrews 13:8) He gave that sinful woman a new beginning. He gave that imperfect woman a new identity. And He gave that rejected woman a new purpose. That is the gospel of Jesus Christ in action today!

JESUS & YOU

Jesus yearns to take up His place of dignity in you and fulfill His purpose in your life.

I believe that whenever we receive His life, we become changed. He always takes the initiative and we are invited to respond. Respond to the Word of God. Respond to the love of Jesus. Respond to His attitudes and His answers to the questions that concern your life

If you have made mistakes, Jesus would say to you today, "I do not condemn you. Just follow me." You do not need to live one more moment of your life with any sense of guilt or condemnation because of things you have done in the past. Today, Jesus gives you *a new beginning.*

You may feel that you have nothing to offer. You may look at others and think "If I could be like them I would feel better about myself and live differently." You are valuable to Jesus because you are His daughter and He wants you to stand in the full dignity of who you are in Him. Do not be put down by any system or analysis or conclusion that says that you do not count. Jesus Christ says that you do. Do not think about yourself the way others think about you. Your identity is in Jesus Christ.

You may have not yet recognized the purpose for which you were born. We often get so sidetracked just making our own plans and our own statement, taking our own stand and carving out our own place. Many times we can even use our achievements or our academic accomplishments as a way of saying, "Please notice me. I count. I am important." But my sister, unless your purpose and fulfillment are found in the person of Jesus Christ, you will never be satisfied.

You have a purpose that is higher than any activity or secular profession. You have a purpose that is higher than any social level. You have a

purpose that began before the foundation of
the world when God said to himself, "Let's make
people." (Genesis 1:26)

You were in God's mind then, and He had a
plan for you that He has never abandoned. All of
hell and every demon power cannot rob God of
His purpose in you, because you are His creation,
made for His glory in the earth. That purpose will
cause you to wake up in the morning and say
with Paul, "It is no longer I who live, but Christ
lives in me; and the life which I now live in the
flesh I live by faith in the Son of God, who loved
me and gave Himself for me." (Galatians 2:20)

You are the body of Christ in the earth. You
are the holy place of His habitation. You are the
tabernacle of His anointing. You are the dispenser
of His mercy and His grace in this earth. You are
the light of the world. You are the salt of the earth.
You are the preservation. You are the healer. You
are the forgiver. You are the tabernacle that fulfills
God's awesome purpose in the earth today.

You have a purpose. I do not care how young

or old you are, how educated or illiterate you are, or how rich or poor you are. I do not care if you have traveled the world or if you have lived your life in one community. You have a purpose with God and nothing can steal it from you if you will recognize it, and say "Yes, Lord."

Dr. LaDonna Osborn is Vice-President and CEO of OSFO International. She has been involved with her parents, T.L. and Daisy Osborn, on their platforms of world evangelism since she was a child. Her life is a living example of Christ's love for people, and she now carries the gospel into this century's new frontiers including China, Russia, French-speaking Africa and the ex-communist nations of Eurasia.

Dr. LaDonna Osborn in India

Dr. LaDonna Osborn with young underground believers in China, holding a Mandarin translation of T.L. Osborn's book, *Healing the Sick*. (Eyes are covered to conceal identity.)

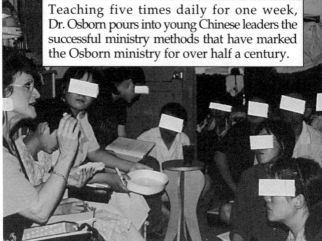

Teaching five times daily for one week, Dr. Osborn pours into young Chinese leaders the successful ministry methods that have marked the Osborn ministry for over half a century.

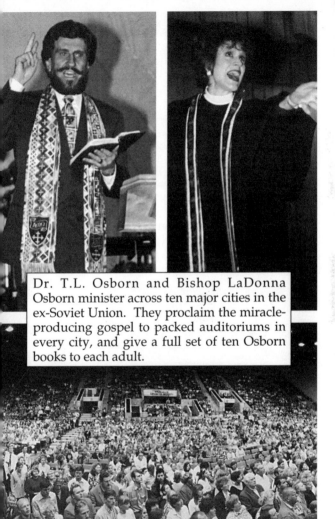

Dr. T.L. Osborn and Bishop LaDonna Osborn minister across ten major cities in the ex-Soviet Union. They proclaim the miracle-producing gospel to packed auditoriums in every city, and give a full set of ten Osborn books to each adult.

Sharing her joy, this woman testifies of her miracle healing from an incurable disease. She tells the people, "Now I know that I am valuable to God. He saw me, He cares for me and He has healed me."

In many nations and different cultures, Bishop Osborn presents the gospel in such a way that each individual can understand God's eternal plan to restore them to dignity, esteem and purpose.

Dr. LaDonna Osborn has set a standard for women in ministry around the world as she continues the gospel legacy of her parents, T.L. and Daisy Osborn.

Dr. Osborn shares the redemptive plan of God's love with pastors in India.

Audience in Hindustan, India

"God has given us the ministry of reconciliation." (II Corinthians 5:18) Wherever Dr. LaDonna Osborn is…in homes, in churches, or on the street…she always brings people to Christ.

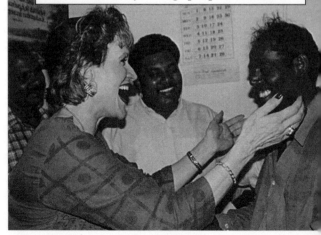

Bishop LaDonna's father, Dr. T.L. Osborn, believes that she is an example for women to emulate. He says, "The power of the gospel is the same when proclaimed by women as when announced by men."

To see a woman preach the gospel with such power, astonishes the people of Kharkov. When Dr. LaDonna Osborn prays, God confirms her ministry with miracles, which is evidence enough to these hardy people that women, as well as men, can serve as Christ's representatives in gospel ministry everywhere.

Mighty miracles confirm the gospel that Bishop LaDonna preaches in Uganda, China, India, Papua New Guinea or wherever people will believe the redemptive message of Christ.

Bishop LaDonna Osborn prays daily that God will bless you with the miracle you need. Write today and share your urgent need.

ABOUT THE AUTHOR

LaDonna
Osborn

LaDonna Osborn is Vice-President
and CEO of OSFO International, the
world missionary church established
by her parents, T.L. and Daisy Osborn,
over 50 years ago.

Dr. Osborn's fresh vision and
leadership, combined with the established ministry and solid experience

of her father, T.L. Osborn, have positioned the organization for expanded outreach into new areas of the world including Russia, French-speaking Africa, Eurasia and the world's largest nation, China. Today, the Osborn ministries share the Gospel of Jesus Christ on every continent, reaching over 80 nations of the world through evangelism, mass-miracle crusades and the distribution of books and literature published in 132 languages.

Her life's passion is to share the Good News of Christ.

She has served as pastor of International Gospel Center in Tulsa, Oklahoma, and is founder and bishop of the International Gospel Center Fellowship of Churches and Ministries, an international network of over 200 pastors and churches.

Dr. LaDonna Osborn is a member of the College of Bishops for the International Communion of Charismatic Churches, which represents over 7,000 pastors, 9,000 churches and more than ten million believers worldwide.

Her ministry, based on the message of redemption, includes preaching, teaching and mass-miracle crusades. She brings a powerful influence to international church ministries, and is widely recognized and respected as a leader in world missions.

Dr. Osborn has four children and 15 grand-children. She and her husband live in Tulsa, Oklahoma.

Notes

Notes

Books by OSFO Publishers

Believers in Action – *Apostolic*

Five Choices for Women Who Win

God's Love Plan

Healing the Sick – *A Living Classic*

How to Be Born Again

Jeus & Women: Answers to Three Big Questions

New Life for Women

Receive Miracle Healing

Soulwinning – *A Classic on Biblical Christianity*

The Best of Life

The Good Life – *A Mini-Bible School*

The Gospel, According to T.L. & Daisy

The Message that Works

The Power of Positive Desire

The Woman Believer

Why? Tragedy Trauma Triumph

Woman Without Limits

Women & Self-Esteem

You Are God's Best

Most Osborn books, audio or video cassettes are available at quantity discounts for bulk purchases, to be used for gifts, resale, ministry outreaches, education or other purposes.

OSFO Publishers, P.O. Box 10, Tulsa, OK 74102 USA
918-743-6231 • FAX 918-749-0339
Email: OSFO@aol.com • www.osborn.org